NATIONAL GEOGRAPHIC

Common Core Readers

Ladders

Watery World

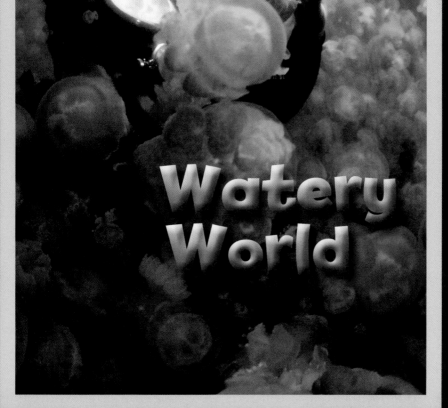

Creatures of the DEEP

by Trudie O'Brien

The whale and the octopus are part of the ocean's watery world. Whales of any **species** are amazing. Just look at their tails, blowholes, flukes, and the way they migrate in pods. Octopuses are a sight with eight arms, suckers, and camouflage skills.

Species of whale and octopus vary in size. One species of octopus can fit in a human hand. Another species is bigger than an adult human. But the blue whale is the largest animal on Earth. Whales and octopuses are different in many ways. They have different life spans. They have differences in the way they look and behave. Dive into the ocean! Let's take a closer look at these amazing animals.

This humpback whale swims near the ocean's surface.

Octopuses, like this giant Pacific octopus, are mollusks. A mollusk is a soft-bodied animal without an internal skeleton.

Ocean Giants

Whales migrate seasonally from one part of the ocean to another part. They travel in a group, or pod. Scientists try to follow whales on their **marine** migrations. It is a good way to learn about each species. How do whales know how to get to their yearly feeding or breeding place? How do whales help their young? Scientists try to find these answers. They track whales to learn more about their life cycles.

Humpbacks in the same area make the same song-like sounds within a season. The songs change from season to season.

blue whale

Blue whales have a streamlined body shape with a broad, flat front part.

Whales use sounds to communicate, or talk, to other whales. Whales are one of the loudest animal species. Humpback whales make song-like sounds. These are messages, but scientists don't understand them.

Scientists also work to make sure certain species of whale stay alive. Blue whales and humpback whales are endangered whale species. There are fewer of these endangered animals now than in the past. Scientists hope the populations of these species will increase.

Whale Size Up

blue whale
Length: 25 to 32 meters (85 to 105 feet)
Weight: up to 181 metric tons (200 tons)

humpback
Length: 14.6 to 19 meters (48 to 62.5 feet)
Weight: about 36 metric tons (40 tons)

gray whale
Length: 12.2 to 15.3 meters (40 to 50 feet)
Weight: 14.5 to 36 metric tons (30 to 40 tons)

bus
Length: about 11 meters (36 feet)
Weight: 9.75 metric tons (10.75 tons)

1 metric ton = 2,204.6 pounds
1 standard ton = 2,000 pounds

humpback whale

gray whale

Gray whales are covered with barnacles and other organisms.

The Ocean's Mammal

Mammals breathe air. So how can a mammal live in the ocean? A whale is a mammal. It breathes air through one or two blowholes on its head. The whale takes a huge breath at the surface of the water. It closes its blowhole and dives down. It can hold its breath for about 10 or 15 minutes. When it comes up for air, it opens its blowhole and exhales. The air it blows can shoot water up to 9.1 meters (30 feet). Whales may dive very deep, but they usually swim near the surface.

Blue, humpback, and gray whales cannot bite or chew. They are **baleen** whales. This means they have a baleen instead of teeth. The baleen is on a whale's upper jaws. The baleen is comb-like plates with bristles. It acts like a strainer.

To feed, a blue or humpback whale gulps a mouthful of water with tiny animals in it. Then its tongue pushes the water through the baleen. This filters and traps tiny animals that the whale swallows. The gray whale gulps water and mud. Then it strains out tiny animals.

Whales have a tail with wide flukes. These are flattened pads that help the whale swim. They move up and down to push the whale forward. The tail helps the whale steer. Whales migrate, or go to warmer waters, in winter. Their tails and flukes help them swim great distances.

Whales work in groups. Humpback whales have worked together to gather fish and to fend off killer sharks.

The cream colored baleen helps this whale feed on tiny krill in ocean water.

Whales breathe
through a blowhole.

Unlike fish tails, whale
flukes fan out sideways.

Female whales give birth to one calf
at a time. Calves continue to grow
and develop for about ten years.

Unusual Mollusks

Octopuses are **mollusks** and **invertebrates.** They do not have skeletons or a backbone. Octopuses have arms with suckers along them. Squid has both arms and tentacles. A tentacle has suckers just at the end point.

Octopuses live between crevices in rocks and coral. Their soft bodies allow them to squeeze in tight spaces, away from predators. They can also hide by changing color and texture.

Whales may live up to 80 years or more. Octopuses have a much shorter life span. Giant Pacific octopuses live for up to five years. The much smaller common octopus lives between one and two years. Male octopuses die after mating. Female octopuses stop eating when they lay eggs. They die after the eggs hatch.

The giant Pacific octopus is the largest octopus species. It can be larger than a human. Many other octopuses are tiny. They could fit on a spoon. And the common octopus species is somewhat in between. Average sizes are about half a meter (1.6 feet).

Giant Pacific octopuses move between shallow waters to depths of 1,500 meters (4,921 feet).

Common octopuses will sometimes collect objects to create gardens or fortresses around their lairs.

Octopus Size Up

bus
Length: about 11 meters (36 feet)
Weight: 9.75 metric tons (10.75 tons)

giant Pacific octopus
Length: 3 to 5 meters (9.75 to 16 feet)
Weight: 10 to 50 kilograms
(22 to 110 pounds)

common octopus
Length: 30.5 to 91.4 centimeters
(12 to 36 inches)
Weight: 3 to 10 kilograms (6.6 to 22 pounds)

Many octopus species hatch and begin their life cycles as tiny larvae. They swim to the surface and start their lives as plankton.

An octopus's ink is a mixture of dark fluid and mucus. This giant Pacific octopus was swimming in waters near British Columbia, Canada.

An octopus can change its color or texture to blend in with its surroundings.

Octopuses: Escape and Attack

Octopuses have large eyes and beak-like mouths. Suckers on their arms have sense organs. These feel, smell, and taste. It's easy to miss an octopus because it can use camouflage to blend in. Its skin can change to match colors and patterns nearby. Special muscles can also change the skin's texture.

If a predator strikes, the octopus shoots water from its siphon, or funnel. The water pushes the octopus forward. The octopus hides its escape by spraying black ink. If it is hard to escape, the octopus can shed an arm. That keeps the predator busy eating while the octopus flees. The octopus regrows the arm later.

The common octopus and the giant Pacific octopus live in warm ocean waters. The giant Pacific octopus lives in the Pacific Ocean near North America, the Aleutian Islands, and Japan.

Whales and octopuses are very smart. But octopuses are the smartest animals without backbones. Their arms allow them to show their smarts. They can use their arms to open jars and solve mazes.

There is a lot of variety within each species of whale or octopus. Octopuses have learned ways to stay safe in the ocean. Whales feed, migrate, and breed. They repeat this pattern for years. Scientists work to protect these two amazing creatures.

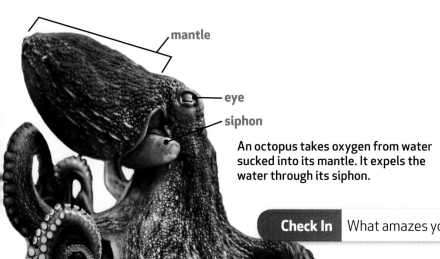

mantle

eye

siphon

An octopus takes oxygen from water sucked into its mantle. It expels the water through its siphon.

Check In What amazes you about whales and octopuses?

GENRE Fantasy

Read to find out how one octopus learns to escape ocean predators.

Sea Warrior

by Hilary Wagner
illustrated by Denis Zilber

Murdina saw a young blue whale coming toward her. His huge mouth was wide open for krill. She hid behind some coral. She had been told that a blue whale would never eat an octopus. Even so, Murdina worried it might just snatch her up by accident. The whale passed by, and Murdina crept out of the shadows. Her name meant sea warrior, but she felt more like a sea coward.

Predator—she didn't like the sound of the word. Her sister said there are predators hiding in the ocean, and an octopus must take care of herself. But she still hadn't learned to camouflage and change shapes. She was sure she was the worst student in the class. Her teacher said that her **instincts** would kick in when she needed them most, but Murdina wasn't so sure. What if her skills didn't come soon enough?

Murdina felt hopeless. She couldn't change color and shape, alter the texture of her skin, or escape in a cloud of ink. Her **species** could do amazing things, but it didn't seem she could. She headed for home, knowing her family could protect her. Suddenly, Murdina saw a hammerhead shark, a fearsome predator. It swam through a cloud of silt. At first, she froze. "Conceal yourself!" she whispered, and looked everywhere.

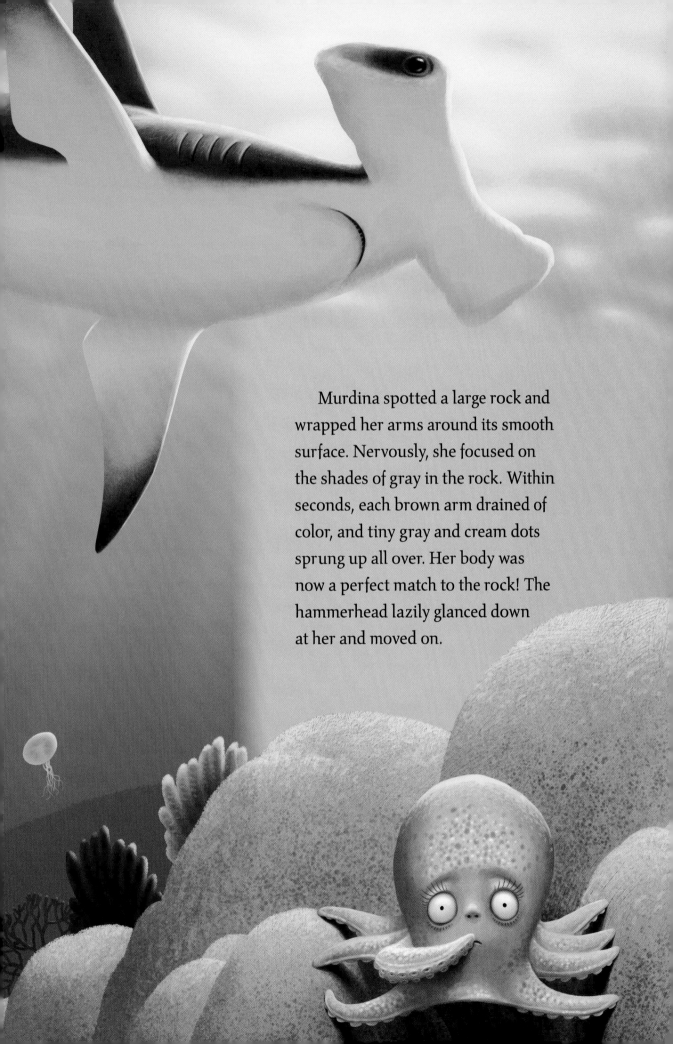

Murdina spotted a large rock and wrapped her arms around its smooth surface. Nervously, she focused on the shades of gray in the rock. Within seconds, each brown arm drained of color, and tiny gray and cream dots sprung up all over. Her body was now a perfect match to the rock! The hammerhead lazily glanced down at her and moved on.

"It worked!" Murdina cried. Her teacher was right about her instincts kicking in. Maybe being so afraid had done the trick, forcing her to take action. Murdina headed home, excited to tell her sister that her camouflage finally worked.

Nearing home, the sea suddenly grew dark. Looking up, Murdina saw a huge boat above her. "A ship!" she said with a gasp. Her teacher had warned the class to stay far away from ships, especially fishing ships that might hunt octopuses.

But Murdina's body was moving towards the surface. She had been caught in a net. She was headed for the fishing boat! The net had holes in it. They were too small for a full-grown octopus, but maybe she could wriggle out. She tried to squish through a hole, but had no luck. Then she forced a jet of water through her funnel. Murdina burst through the hole in the net. She was free! She swam as fast as she could away from the ship.

Murdina felt a rush of excitement. Her sister would be proud. She did have octopus instincts. She spun in a circle, smiling, when she heard a low, slithery voice behind her. "Why so happy young one? What is such a delicious octopus celebrating?"

Murdina turned to see a moray eel. Its sharp teeth were gleaming. "Don't be afraid. I don't want to hurt you," it said with an oily grin.

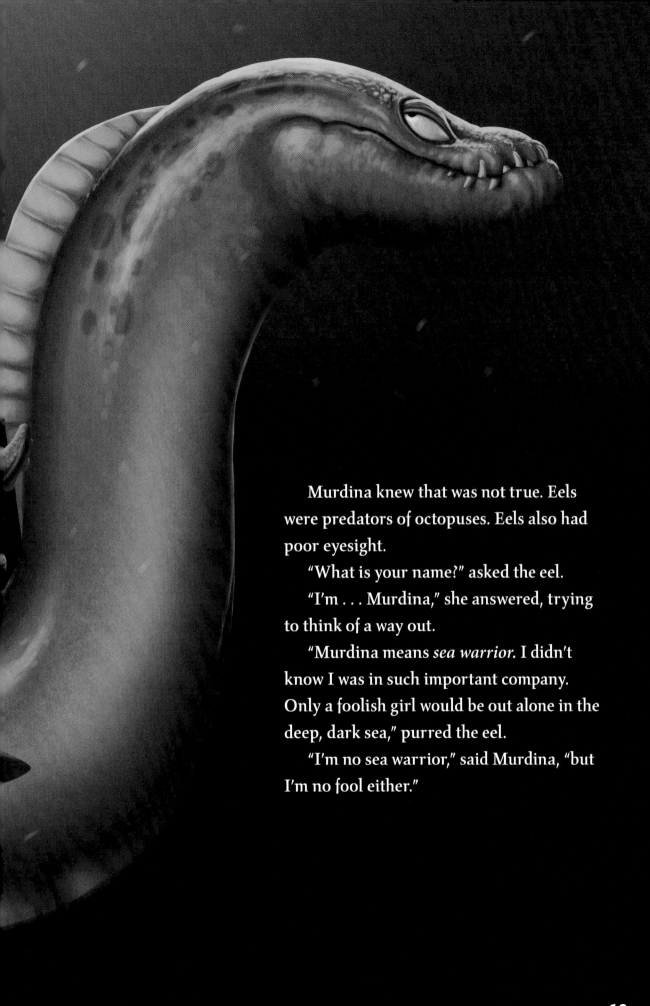

Murdina knew that was not true. Eels were predators of octopuses. Eels also had poor eyesight.

"What is your name?" asked the eel.

"I'm . . . Murdina," she answered, trying to think of a way out.

"Murdina means *sea warrior*. I didn't know I was in such important company. Only a foolish girl would be out alone in the deep, dark sea," purred the eel.

"I'm no sea warrior," said Murdina, "but I'm no fool either."

Looking at a sea plant, Murdina had an idea.
She pushed a jet of ink into the eel's face. She swam
through the black cloud of ink, grabbing onto the base
of a ruffled red kelp. Her skin quickly changed to the
exact color of the kelp. She waved her arms like the
kelp's frilly blades. "Where did you go?" the eel called
out crossly. The eel glided by, unaware that Murdina
was hidden in the kelp.

The eel finally gave up looking for her and swam away. Murdina was now aware she needed to save her joy until she was safe at home. Predators were everywhere. No wonder the octopuses had developed such amazing skills. Murdina finally arrived at their **marine** burrow. Murdina's sister looked at her curiously. "Something's changed about you," she said. "You look like a great warrior returning from battle."

"Let's go inside," said Murdina. "I'll tell you all about it."

Check In   What animal behaviors saved Murdina from ocean predators?

21

Charlie's Swim

by Hilary Wagner
illustrated by Paule Trudel Bellemare

Charlie rolled out of bed and walked to the window of the hotel room. He looked out at the ocean dancing up and down the shoreline. He'd been waiting for this day— his twelfth birthday. For his present, his older brother Seth was taking him blue whale watching. Charlie had been studying them in school and now he would get to see real blue whales, not just pictures of the **species**. He was relieved Seth had agreed. After all, he needed to see the real thing if he was to become a **marine biologist**.

The blue whale is the largest living creature on Earth, with a life span of around eighty years. Weighing a huge 200 tons, the size of a blue whale was staggering, but, Charlie thought, maybe even the blue whale felt tiny in the vast sea. Softly, he opened up the sliding glass door and went out onto the beach, sand particles sticking to his feet. The sound of the ocean gently hitting the shore was like a rhythmic lullaby. It reminded him of his mother singing to him when he was a child. He wondered if young whales liked the sound, too.

As Charlie watched the frothy waves, a sound filled the air, coming from the ocean. It sounded like a tuba, only lower in pitch and much, much louder—it was the call of the blue whale! Charlie ran to the water's edge, the waves reaching his toes. He knew he shouldn't go this far out on his own, but something told him he'd be fine. He took a step farther into the water, the cuffs of his pajama pants getting soaked. He saw something gliding through the water, the top of its rounded body breaking the water's surface.

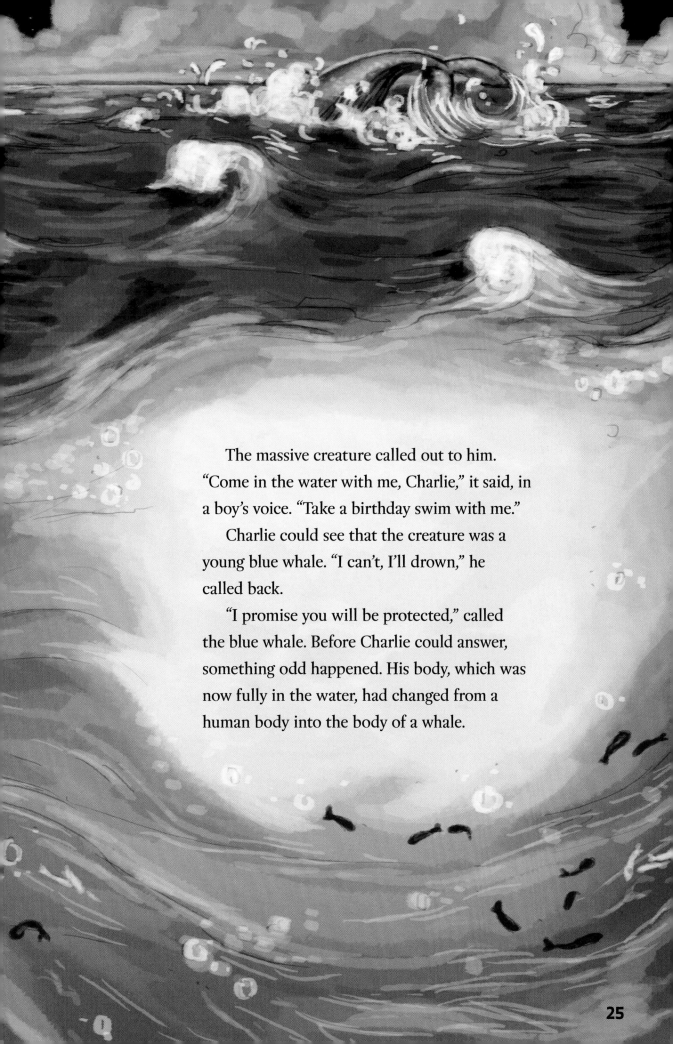

The massive creature called out to him. "Come in the water with me, Charlie," it said, in a boy's voice. "Take a birthday swim with me."

Charlie could see that the creature was a young blue whale. "I can't, I'll drown," he called back.

"I promise you will be protected," called the blue whale. Before Charlie could answer, something odd happened. His body, which was now fully in the water, had changed from a human body into the body of a whale.

Charlie dove after the other blue whale, water rushing around his newly-formed fins and tail. "Wait for me!" he called. "What's your name?"

"I'm Azul," said the whale.

"Where are you headed, Azul?" asked Charlie, his eyes widening at his new friend.

"My parents said it's time to go the **Costa Rica Dome**," Azul replied. Charlie spotted two fully-grown blue whales trailing them in the distance. "This is my first winter there; it stays warmer there than California, and my older brothers say the water has lots of krill."

"I know what krill is," said Charlie. "It's the miniature shrimp-like animal you eat."

Azul bellowed with laughter. "Well, you eat it too, for now, Charlie!"

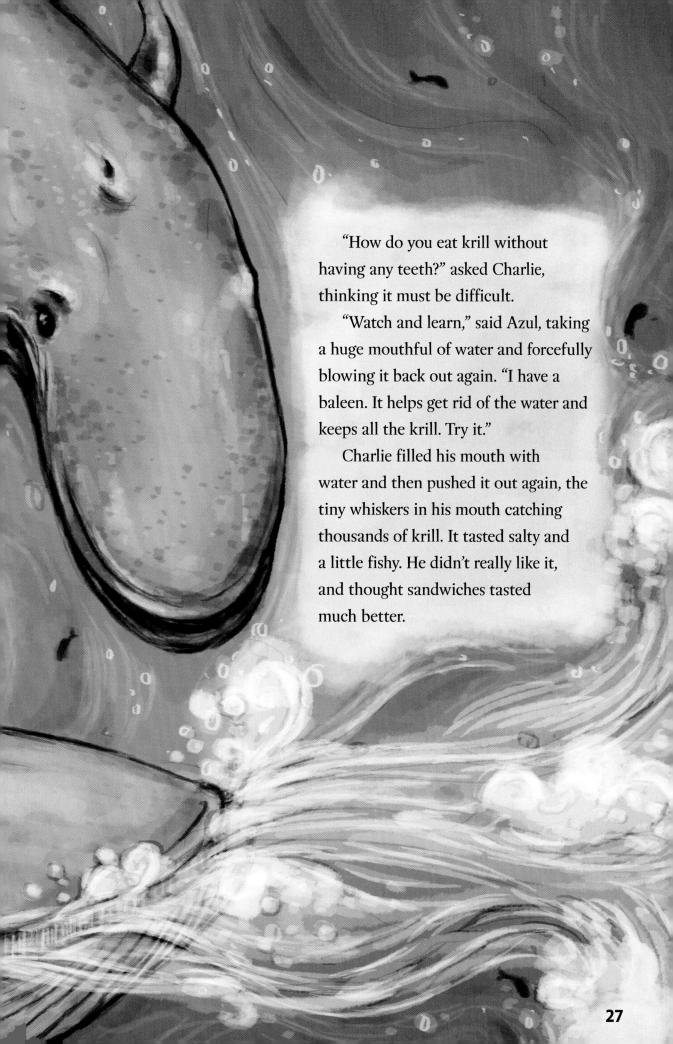

"How do you eat krill without having any teeth?" asked Charlie, thinking it must be difficult.

"Watch and learn," said Azul, taking a huge mouthful of water and forcefully blowing it back out again. "I have a baleen. It helps get rid of the water and keeps all the krill. Try it."

Charlie filled his mouth with water and then pushed it out again, the tiny whiskers in his mouth catching thousands of krill. It tasted salty and a little fishy. He didn't really like it, and thought sandwiches tasted much better.

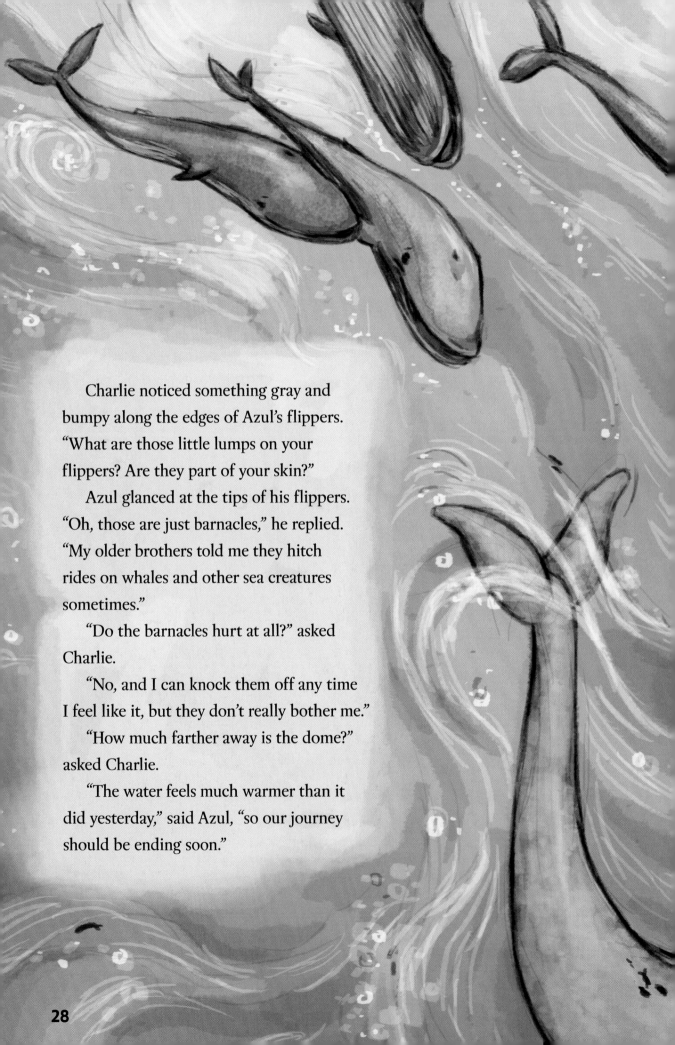

Charlie noticed something gray and bumpy along the edges of Azul's flippers. "What are those little lumps on your flippers? Are they part of your skin?"

Azul glanced at the tips of his flippers. "Oh, those are just barnacles," he replied. "My older brothers told me they hitch rides on whales and other sea creatures sometimes."

"Do the barnacles hurt at all?" asked Charlie.

"No, and I can knock them off any time I feel like it, but they don't really bother me."

"How much farther away is the dome?" asked Charlie.

"The water feels much warmer than it did yesterday," said Azul, "so our journey should be ending soon."

"Won't you miss your older brothers in the California waters?" asked Charlie, thinking how much he'd miss Seth if he couldn't see him for an entire winter.

Twisting around, Azul pointed with his massive snout. Charlie gazed upon a whole pod of young blue whales, traveling behind Azul's parents. "They've all come with you?" he asked in disbelief.

"My parents said they've got a big surprise for us, so this year we all decided to travel to the Dome together," said Azul. "Traveling as a pod, or group, protects us from the orcas too. Sometimes they attack the younger whales. Dad always says there is safety in numbers."

It was hard to believe that the largest creature in the sea could be at risk from predators of any kind. After today, though, Charlie supposed anything was possible.

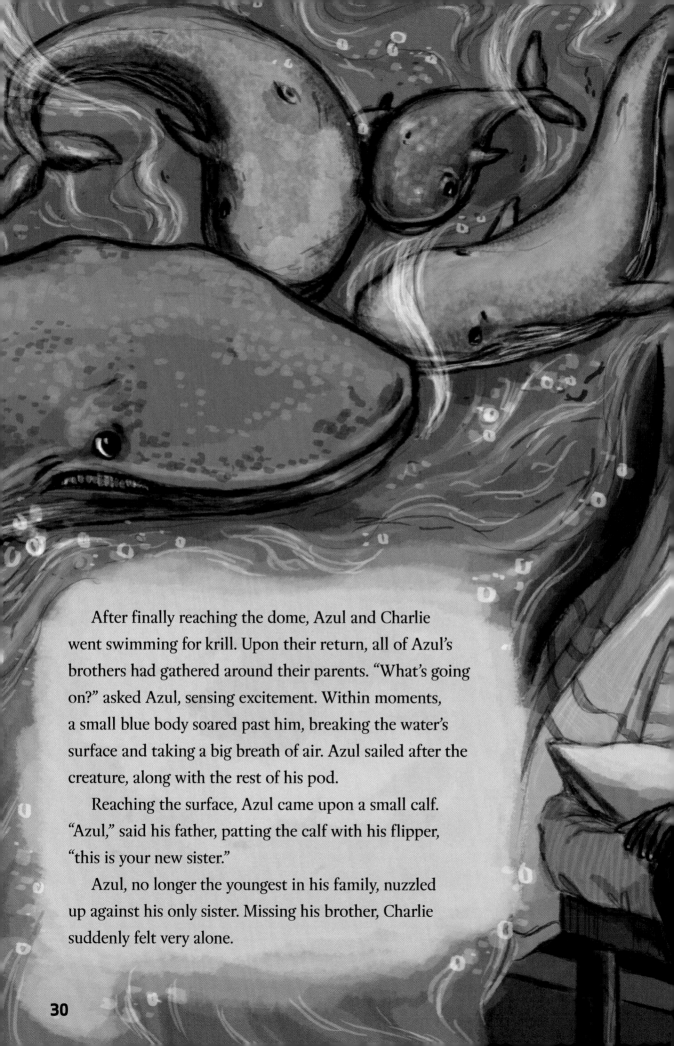

After finally reaching the dome, Azul and Charlie went swimming for krill. Upon their return, all of Azul's brothers had gathered around their parents. "What's going on?" asked Azul, sensing excitement. Within moments, a small blue body soared past him, breaking the water's surface and taking a big breath of air. Azul sailed after the creature, along with the rest of his pod.

Reaching the surface, Azul came upon a small calf. "Azul," said his father, patting the calf with his flipper, "this is your new sister."

Azul, no longer the youngest in his family, nuzzled up against his only sister. Missing his brother, Charlie suddenly felt very alone.

Charlie awoke to the feeling of gentle nudging against his arm. "Charlie, it's time to wake up." He sat up in bed and looked at Seth, who smiled at him with sleepy eyes. "Hey, little brother, it's your birthday, time to get up and see the whales," said Seth.

Everything had seemed so real, thought Charlie, remembering how it felt to be a whale, swimming in the ocean depths with Azul. For a moment, he was sad, realizing it was only a dream.

Seth ruffled Charlie's hair. "You sure slept late for a budding marine biologist so eager to meet the whales."

Thinking back on the dream, Charlie smiled at his brother.

"Oh, I'm ready to see them," Charlie said, but he already felt like he knew them pretty well.

Check In What surprise did Azul's parents have for him?

31

Discuss Compare and Contrast

1. What connections can you make between the three pieces in *Watery World*? How are the pieces related?

2. Compare and contrast the two stories, "Sea Warrior" and "Charlie's Swim."

3. How are the topics of the two stories alike and different?

4. What information did you learn about the size of whales and octopuses? Compare the two animals.

5. What questions do you still have about animal life in the ocean?